Richard Ryan

Ledges

Poetry Ireland Editions

The Dolmen Press

Set in Times Roman type and printed and published at The Dolmen Press Limited, 8 Herbert Place, Dublin 2 in the Republic of Ireland.

Distributed outside Ireland, except in Canada and in the United States of America by Oxford University Press.

SBN 19 647549 X

Acknowledgements

Some of these poems have appeared in the following journals: Broadsheet; Nusight; Poetry Workshop Broadsheet; The Irish Press; The Irish Times; St. Stephen's *and* Steppenwolfe (Omaha).

for my mother

Contents

'She dwelleth and abideth upon the rock.
Her children also suck up blood.'

JOB

Cliff-Climbing

Above the ordered plain of insect
Cattle, farms and tiny contoured
Fields, its blind head ringed with mist:
The monstrous cliff. A wall against the sun.

Where, at its most sheer, by rain,
By wind whipped bald as bone, clinging —
A man, clockwork fingers, clockwork feet
Testing for hold. Motion ceases . . .

Eyes squeezed tight, his brain scrabbles with fear.
Tales of other casualties cram into his head —
Picked piecemeal from the rocks a mile
Below, their broken brains, hands, feet

Reconstructed like jigsaws, all with the same
Answer: to see the sun cliff-climbers must become,
Not better men, but something more or something
Less than men. And so, brainless, fly-like

His fingers stir again, walk up the wall, find,
Clamp upon a knob of rock that was not there
Before, drag him higher and a ledge
Waits; he rests, then continues to climb.

Building

for Maurice and Pauline Sweeney

April,
         rain-dance
in tinkling tree-light,
              goldcrest
talking to himself,
stealing spiders' webs,
moss, feather another fellow
lost — tic, tic, ch-ch-ch-ch-ch!
bothered, getting hit
with rain-drops, but
the wife waits, fattening —
chur-r-r, chur-r-r! eggs
soon, globes of vein,
blood, beginnings of brain.
hei! hei! hei! —
the wind!
              build well.

The Thrush's Nest

for Michael Kinsella

Bramble, like barbed wire,
Stitches the thicket tight, laces
A net of leaves against the
Sun: only the birds can pass.

Pinned high where the twigs
Cross, it shapes from a blur;
Still heart of the bush, darkness
Parts slowly to let it through.

Her black pebble-eyes dazed
With waiting, the mother snaps
Alive at my presence, grabs
Air, screaming — reveals her shining

Hoard: luminous with heat,
Four freckled ovals of perfect
Sky, the skin of one threaded
With cracks — pulsing with life.

A Heap of Stones

1 FAMINE VILLAGE
for Joy McGloin   d. 1969

This maze of stones which the wind cuts and hones
Smooth, down, was in another century
The homes of famine fishermen, whose bones

Long buried, now without a memory,
Have fertilised this bramble wilderness
Of grass and thistle reaching to the knee,

Which press upwards and thicken and caress
The naked chimneys and the broken walls
Which breathe the sea-mist and the emptiness.

Where once children played, now only gulls' calls
Echo and die slowly across the wide
Wild curve of sand to where the mountain falls

Into the sea. The land was bad — they tried
To work the tide; they lived a life-long fight
To live and lost to graves on Slieve More's side.

Now a grey rain thickens the fading light.
Slowly the ruins become the mist and
Merge silently with the descending night.

I asked directions
at a farmhouse door:
they pointed to a field
high on the hillside
where they said
the Giant's Grave
stood, and waited,
watching by their gate,
an old man
and his wife, watching
till I turned the road,
wondering perhaps why
a man would climb
half a mountain to see
a heap of stones.

Over the ditch and through
the rising bog spotted
with tiny spits of wild cotton
I moved, a mile
an hour, until the land
below became a mood,
long shadows sweeping
inland, eating light . . .

Armed with bright pictures
of club and claw
I searched until suddenly
it grinned at me:
filling the hole in a crazy hedge
it overflowed into the field —
great tables impaled
upon a pencil of stone;

14

a tabernacle of ancient death
dug deep as an evil eye
in the skull of the hill.
I banished urgent images
from my downward path and one
by one unclenched
the stone cold fingers round my brain.

3 DUGORT

There are two graveyards
there: one Catholic
and still stoutly respectable —
almost living, one might say.
On holy-days, after Mass,
the children run
over silent stones
and play with guns among graves
bearing their own names...

The family rosary
remembers those bones
and nightly knits
a tapestry as safe
and sure as the promise
which will one day crack
and tumble those earthly stones.

The old churchyard beside the mountain and the sea
knows no children, but noisy rooks and wind
and silence and scarce a living memory;
these other graves, beneath the grey walls and the trees,
await eternity with a crumbling, Protestant dignity.

15

4 CLIFF WALK — DUN AENGUS

for Desirée Moorehead

Up there the wind
is wet and chilled
as mountain rain;
grey ribs of stone
ripple in antique
strategy and tighten
to the edge. Below,

the sea. From the lip
of the cliff my mind
plummets: waves
heave, burst
wide and bleed
backwards down long
knives of rock.

But wind and sea
know nothing of assault

and bite the rockjaws
now as then when,
while from the East
a foreign priest strode
West, kings constructed
walls to fight for fields
and did not recognise the enemy.

A hedge of shields, a wall
could turn a spear, but not the dawn:

Thin grains of day
spilled pale and spread
westward licking night
over the cliffs and bundled
snakes, religion, runes
into the seavaults
somewhere under the sunset.

5 MUSHROOM PICKING — LIECHTENSTEIN

I

Blond cornfields only
Slowly surrender their
Geometry to threads of pine
That climb skyhigh with me
Against the sky, spreading
Like mist across rocky stone
To lock forever a web of
Night against day.

Legend lives here: through
Mile high mountains echo
The inaudible horns of
Secrecy, a windchipped music
Tingling through the harpstrings
Of my brain — this, it
Whispers, is where myth begins,
And perhaps ends . . .

II

Leaving the track with baskets, I
Collect: in the forest halls
Humped under dead leaves or
Chasing pagan circles around the black
Pillars of trees, their skins
Wet with clay, they squat
Like tiny blank eyeballs staring
From a Gothic or Grimm world

Until, with broken
Necks, white dwarf blood
Clotting tiny tendrils, they
lie in heaps, recede
Then grow again, become
Dead mushrooms, defined,
Contained by the habitual,
The walls of a box.

6 KNOCKMANY

for John Montague

In slow procession
trees ascend
the hill, enter
the mist-held ring
to crowd, chanting,
around the silent
hive of stones.

Giant tree-priests,
slowly they rock
in prayer; searching
the earth long root
veins writhe down-
ward, probing
for blood the deep

hill's heart. As
the quick sap stirs,
runnels upward
through trunk and
thigh, filling
with its white life
the glistening loins,

louder the branches,
bone-hard arms
dipping, digging
up air, moan —
mad with certainty —
as the mist,
prised up like a stone,

reveals a monstrous
shadow rising, rising
through the forked, skinless
fingers — the
swaying trees lean
forward, clutching the twitching
shape, humming . . . humming . . .

7 VIKING DEPOSITS

I Museum

Bog fruit;
skinless, a
scrap of hair
and rotted
sword, contour
of skull; the
glass casket,
electric light:
the shape
roughly human.

II Trelleborg

Silence. Cloud
hand shadows
grapple bald walls
and climb the
wind, walk over
Trelleborg;
deft sheep topple
dew-drops down
mounds: the silence,
so, is not soundless . . .

III   Runestone

Chant round
red fire,
flicker of lips
and toad
under wet stone:
blob eye
and ticking
heart slowly
staring the sun
down . . .

IV   The brain

To mere, iron
on bone, to
mood mind
pulls the eye:
lithe-thighed
they step at dawn —
ravens wind high
and wait — in
the first crash
men fall . . .

bog fruit;
skinless, a
scrap . . .

Father of Famine

for Liam O'Flaherty

Shadow boxer, fighting
Man, old locust
Eater, bruised waxwing
Of the nest of dust;
O feeder of honey to the dead —
Mon père,
I would be led:
Must I neglect food to know hunger?

Dice

for Matthew

The tip flick of the thin
steel finger into first
slams wet wheels scream spinning
from the mouth of the pub
the leaping headlights pick
ing slipping between streets
the two cars locked by twin
light shafts one makes a break
loses the road mad search
lights spin skyhigh pinpoint
a wall and flesh slaps stone.

the single tear
of a street light hangs
while tired tyres
spin to a
stop.

Behind the Wall

I

Muscle bunches. Wild heart
swings, slaps his chest. Eyelids

skid back. Mad with knowledge
eyes grip, rake the forest —

silence. Steam climbs the light,
a blood bird needles green . . .

This the sun saw: bullet rod bone.

In the dying, head full of light,
of light, toppling to stop, a

monkey leaps, screaming, its half-
brain snapping with fear, toppling

to stop. The jungle settles
down, begins again to sweat . . .

II

I died. Taken by all,
Buried. Behind the wall

Of clay skin wafers, peels
From bone. Wood rots; bone seals

The brain in death. Above
Flowers, lifebelts of love,

Lie, drink the rain and die.
The earth, a great blind eye,

Turns, dead in a skull sky.

III

The theme dying is the theme:
not what is in
the grave,
but what went in.
And so the crazy man
raked clay on the dead
eye.
That stopped the stare.

i.e., this is taught
widely, so —
unless all are —
I am not mad
and, either way,
fit where I must:
among the sane,
the mad — one word?

The eye swivels again,
impales the tongue.
Speechless,
only one way:
perhaps
there is
no
word.

Deafness

for my sister

It is when I hear Mozart,
some birds, the scraping
of wind through pine and
she is there; sounds crowd
round her silence like clay.

It is then I hear the note —
an inkling of the sound
of death: not the mere being
without, but the not knowing,
at all...

School Girl

1 SCHOOL GIRL

Again you ride my mind.
This time I grip my hooks,
Grapple and hold. You

Come: a beach curves,
Blurs across my sight and
Clears under the sun.
Low tide; small waves
Eyelash the sand: you
Run, crushed spray lacing
Your thighs, your body
Hot, sunburnt. Touching,
We kiss behind the wind,
Your mouth is salt and

Stop! My line, stiff
As driftwood, has
Snapped — my hooks
Trail in the sand.
The sun goes out.

2 DO YOU REMEMBER?

I touched you
it was
in the wood
under a black
bird's nest
and there was
your eyes and mine.

29

I remember
this but not
better than
the four green
eggs we looked
at after
and the sun
like leaves
on the dead leaves
where we were.

I've been back there

and the buzz-saw
is busy
in the trees now
not a blackbird
and there will
be houses
there they said
they will
build houses on
the wood

and my girl
friend and I
walk on
sawdust that
was your wood
and mine.

3 A LATE EXPLANATION

(Sometimes the bucket
draws not only
clear water from
the well . . .)

Almost four years.
Some parts of you I
Pick at will — your
Crow-dark hair, those
Hands, the first tiny
Experiments . . . But

Here I passed by chance.
The old place shapes you
Suddenly: stone shed
For tourists, or lovers;
That seasucked tongue of rock
And, still, the rain. Yes

Memory peels back. The
Bad Winter: my mind
Rocked on its rails of
Logic, German books, that
Death. Jesus too was dying
In my brain: the night

We talked even the stars
Pinned over Howth rebuked
The Cross. In this you were
With me, me without you:
Your arms were teeth
I found around my soul.

I tried to tell.
You heard, held me,
Spoke of marriage, children:
My tongue broke in your mouth!

4 ON HEARING OF AN ENGAGEMENT

Will you ever go
away? certain
places, songs lump
in my brain; you
linger in them like
mist threading a glen
out of the sun's

eye. But this I can
control: I would
not have the past
become a jaw, in
ritual to file
the teeth which could —
and did — eat the heart

out. No, that
I can control.
It is the since
I do not know: small
scraps of news, your health,
the vague particulars; now this.
I do not know you anymore, but

will you ever go ... ?

I remember
                    I
yes
        head
and behind
the eyes   skin-
taste   touch
                you
remember

            yes I
know it was
        then

            but
remember when
        yes
it was

            but
what
        is that
O perfect
            dome of
silence
doing there that
        you wear
under
        your
    dress
                there

Wolf-Hour

The brain lurches
suddenly, cables of sleep
snapping like veins, and
the claws hike mercilessly
closer, sharp as scalpels,
tearing the will like cobwebs

down. The old, faceless
monsters from childhood, now
suddenly I recognise them all
as, swaying giddily past
in a colourless pageant of horror,
of truth, each one glides near

(peering sockets, mouth
of grinning bone) and one
by one they go — this face
and that, all harmed by
cruelty, denial, betrayal:
old splinters buried in the heart.

Ghost-like they pass and fade
to leave only darkness
and bitter memory rising,
filling the brain as it rocks
from hurt to hurt, waiting for light,
a numb dome of bone in the dark.

Foundations

for Margaret

Our dog screamed, snapped under the wheel
And died. Hurt floods our mind: I feel

The words straddle my tongue —'darling
He felt no . . . .' too easy! The wing

Of death kills speech. But all deaths die —
The brain revives; it must. Only

The helplessness remains: in it
Our strength. The thin wicks twine and, lit

Again, burn down as one. The darkness glows.

Hawk

'Hafuc sceal on glófe wilde gewunian ...'
GNOMIC VERSES

Like teeth on tongue,
the mailed claw
dents (but will not
bruise) the blue-
veined lady's wrist:
stone eye and clicking
beak proclaim his strength.

At the stirring
of seasons or
the sight of blood —
flash of a robin's
breast in snow —
the armoured feathers
flex, tremble the air

but will not launch
those iron claws:
morsels may increase
the appetite, but
a wise hawk
knows where his dinner
is, and must obey.

How This Poem Happened

The city crouched in darkness,
so, words on my mind, I
found the fields, some trees:

White skin of the moon
impaled upon pine, its face
repeated palely on the lake's
face: they touch, trembling.

Colourless smell of dawn.
The lake breathes soundlessly
across the wet grey fields —
long tentacles of mist probing
the woods, streaking the dark
trees white: night stirs, restless.

Startled, a fox flames
from bramble, burns a hole
into the dark and fires
the gathered twigs behind
my brain: with threads
of silk my pen begins
to stitch. Slowly the darkness
parts until, somewhere, the birds
begin; light props the trees
against the day: morning.